The **SPIRIT** *of* STEAM

The SPIRIT of STEAM

The Golden Age of North American Steam

WILLIAM L. WITHUHN

SMITHMARK

This book is dedicated to Lloyd M. Arkinstall —
engineer, artist, raconteur, teacher, friend

This edition published in 1995 by
SMITHMARK Publishers Inc.,
16 East 32nd Street,
New York, NY 10016.

9 8 7 6 5 4 3 2

SMITHMARK books are available for bulk purchase for sales promotion and
premium use. For details write or call the manager of special sales,
SMITHMARK Publishers Inc.,
16 East 32nd Street, New York,
NY 10016; (212) 532-6600.

ISBN 0-8317-5511-3

Printed in Singapore.

CREDITS
Project Editors: Will Steeds/Tony Hall
Editor: Anthony Lambert
Designer: John Heritage
Filmset: Bookworm Typesetting, England
Color Reproduction: P&W Graphics Pte Ltd, Singapore

All correspondence concerning the content of this volume should be
addressed to Salamander Books Ltd., 129-137 York Way, London N7 9LG,
United Kingdom.

FRONT ENDPAPERS: — *Steam and electric locomotives congregate in Montana on
the Milwaukee Road in the late 1940s; photo by Philip Hastings, courtesy of
Marian Hastings.*

BACK ENDPAPERS: — *Five-year-old Pam Hastings, the photographer's daughter,
regards a Western Maryland Ry. locomotive in Baltimore in 1952, photo
courtesy of Marian Hastings.*

PAGE 1: — *Study of a steam locomotive driving wheel and side rod, by
Wilton Tifft.*

PAGE 2: — *Two Denver & Rio Grande Western narrow-gauge locomotives work
upgrade in Colorado in a late 1950s photo by Ron Ziel.*

PAGE 4: — *On the preserved Nevada Northern Ry., photographer Oren Helbok
found No. 40 by the East Ely, Nevada, coaling tower in 1987.*

CONTENTS

FOREWORD

The idea of doing a book like this – a collection of images from the height of the steam era on North American railroads – has appealed to me for a long time. But I did not want to do a book just for railroad buffs. To me, the challenge that matters for any historian, on any subject, is reaching the non-specialized, *general public*.

Fine photo books exist designed for railroad fans; what is rare are such books having general appeal, books which are specifically designed for readers with perhaps a casual interest but who are put off by the arcane vocabulary, the images without context, and the fixation on mechanical details that railfans so love. If we as railfans (and I am certainly one) bear an 'image' problem, it is in large measure due to our inability to get outside ourselves, to get beyond our specialized lore and to describe and portray our subject in broader, more universal terms that will appeal to wider audiences.

Modern audiences live in a much more visually-oriented world than did their parents or grandparents. Today, even academic historians understand better the unique power of the image as primary evidence – evidence that is indispensable to social history and which allows us to appreciate parts of the past otherwise unknowable. But context must be provided; just as with any artifact from history, pictures do not just speak for themselves. For me, a key way to achieve context is with other pictures. A pretty image by itself is relatively meaningless; seen with a series of related pictures, an image can convey understanding in a way it can not do alone.

In this book, the pictures were chosen in a very conscious way to illustrate selected aspects of the railroad story in North America from the 1920s through the 1950s. The chapter introductions are important, providing the contextual frame for the photographs. But it is the pictures themselves that carry the story; the text and captions 'illustrate' the photographs, rather than the other way around.

The author owes debts to many people who helped him. Thanks are due to Will Steeds, who originally conceived this book, and to editor Tony Hall and to designer John Heritage.

Photographers who generously shared the work they have done over many years include Glenn Beier, Shirley Burman, Jim Gallagher, John Gruber, John Helbok, Oren Helbok, Joel Jensen, Dick Kindig, Jim Shaughnessy, Dick Steinheimer, Wilton Tifft, Jeff Tinsley, and Ron Ziel. Special thanks go to Marian Hastings, for sharing the work of her husband, Phil.

Outstanding help in providing photographs, in picture identification, and in other ways came from Peter Barton at the Railroaders' Memorial Museum, Altoona, Pa.; Seth Bramson, Miami, Fla.; Jim Boyd of Railfan & Railroad magazine; Bob

William L. Withuhn is Curator of Transportation, Smithsonian Institution. He was a shortline railroad manager and has run a variety of steam locomotives since 1966. Here, in 1994, he is running a train at the Steamtown National Historic Site, Scranton, Pa.

Emerson, Bob Linden, and Ken Riegel at the Railroad Museum of Pennsylvania, Strasburg; John Hankey at the University of Chicago; Joyce Koeneman at the Association of American Railroads, Washington; Jerry Kuncio at the B&O Railroad Museum, Baltimore; Stephen Lyons of the Canadian Pacific Archive, Montreal; Bob Patterson at the Steamtown National Historic Site, Scranton, Pa.; Bill Schafer at the Norfolk Southern Corporation, Norfolk; Don Snoddy and Bill Kratville of the Union Pacific Railroad Museum, Omaha; Mark Smith of Great Eastern Publishing Co., Richmond, Vt.; and Jack White, Roger White, and Bill Worthington at the Smithsonian Institution, Washington. My appreciation goes to all.

INTRODUCTION

This is a book for people who like trains – but who are not attracted to the specialized language and interests of railroad buffs. This is a book that attempts to describe for a general readership, through pictures and focused text, something about trains in the United States and Canada from the 1920s through the 1950s – the final years in which railroads were a highly visible and consequential part of everyday life.

Today, in the public consciousness, railroads are part of the plumbing of society – part of our 'infrastructure' – and taken for granted by most of us, if they are noticed at all. Modern railroads play their economic role efficiently and well, and they are about as interesting to observe as conveyor belts. It was not always so. In the steam era, trains were intrinsically interesting to watch.

What was the 'spirit' of steam railroading? Where did that intrinsic interest come from? The problem today, in trying to recapture the spirit of railroading from a half-century ago, is that the machines – the big and often spectacular locomotives and trains from those days – are not enough. The context is missing. In fact, I would argue, the interest one might have in trains, either then or today, is not really intrinsic at all but entirely dependent on context.

Those who see trains out of a personal interest first developed in the 1940s or 1950s may have difficulty understanding the sensibilities of most people living today. To some of us, a steam locomotive may be a glorious creation. But, in truth, a steam locomotive

Photographer Frank Quin made this picture in the 1940s at Johnsonville, New York, on the Boston & Maine Railroad. Here is the train in one of its main functions: connecting small-town America with the rest of the world. Steam condenses in the cold air.

is brutal, ugly, spews polluting exhaust seemingly out of all proportion to its size, and is a product of an entirely different industrial era than that of today's high-precision, computer-directed machinery. Certainly that stark contrast, in itself, with today's cleanly efficient mechanical contrivances, is part of steam's appeal to many. But again, it is not enough.

Modern railroads… are about as interesting to observe as conveyor belts.

The missing context is people. The appeal of trains in the steam age was based not on the big machines but on the human beings – the people who ran the trains, the people who used the trains, and their human purposes in doing so. People were the 'spirit,' not the machines.

Let me elaborate. When I was growing up, trains were indeed the 'biggest and baddest' things around (to use my eleven-year-old's current phrase). But more: in contrast to cars and airplanes and other things in which small boys were also passionately inter-

Photographer Dick Kindig caught the streamlined 'Cincinnatian' of the Baltimore & Ohio Railroad, Train No. 76, climbing Cranberry Grade near Amblersburg, West Virginia, in Fall 1948. The fireman regards the camera, as he works his coal stoker and boiler-water systems.

ested, trains were clearly more important to the way the rest of the world worked. Trains brought everything into town: one's food, Dad's new car, most things on store shelves, heavy machinery, express boxes and packages, the mail, Grandma on a visit, Dad back from a trip. A lot of adults in town had relationships with the railroad – as employees, as travelers, as business owners and farmers relying on the railroad. Trains were part of life, more important than the weather. Now, that is context.

And there was more. The trains were big, all right, but real people were in charge. In the railroad scene, the canard about machines dominating people was obviously nonsense. The skill of railroad people was so evident; their intense pride – sometimes swaggering, usually quiet – was so easily perceived.

The longest freight train was dominated by an engineer, one who could move those thousands of tons either brutally or delicately, at will. The fastest passenger train was utterly dependent on the man who could roll it easily into town, stop it gently on a dime, and take it gently off again, all to a precision as fine as a ballet. The dispatcher was so clearly in command of complexities beyond comprehension. The hostlers and mechanics so clearly handled their huge charges as easily as the guys at the corner gas station handled my dad's lube job. Even the baggage men had an air of important tasks, although simple, done well. Maybe, it occurred to me later, these people knew that the roles they played were essential ones.

An essential truth is that most people are interested in people, not in machines.

By the early 1950s, as the relative importance of railroads waned and as they began the severe economic slide from which they would not recover until the mid-1980s, their employees endured increasing public scorn. If the 1920–50 period was a 'golden age' – and it certainly was in the development of the North American steam locomotive – the thirty years after 1950 saw railroads nearly disappear. To me it seemed that railroaders had fallen in public esteem perhaps, but they had not given up any of the wonderful skills, or pride, that had originally attracted me. Their dignity, it struck me, was not something defined by mere public accolade, but by their own quiet fortitude.

Context: that is what is missing today when we look at a picture of a train from fifty years ago. The train's essential public role is missing; the people involved and their skills are missing. In most of the pictures in this book, these elements are missing. One must add the context to give these pictures any meaning, and therefore any interest, at all. And the most important elements of context are never specific to any given picture, able to be revealed in a short caption. Reflection on things not in the picture is always required.

An essential truth is that most people are interested in people, not in machines. A picture of a machine is one thing, but even the most beautifully restored steam locomotive in action today, able to steam and to run, showing off its fascinating rhythms and counter-rhythms, is just a machine to most of us – at best, a sort of animated industrial sculpture. It is the people associated with the machine that must give it meaning. To the railroad fan, the contextual human meaning seems unimportant to him, but it is there nonetheless, hidden in the recesses of memory. The machine's true meaning, for him, is hidden in the human associations that went along on his first train ride long before, or in the human associations he made for himself. A machine, by and of itself, has no meaning.

There is, however, a still larger context. That context is the role

From the archive of Ron Ziel comes this shot of a K4-type locomotive on the Long Island Rail Road in 1949, at Cold Spring Harbor, New York. The fireman has seen the photographer and has added more coal than his fire needs, unduly darkening the smoke.

of railroads in the growth and development of nations. In that regard, we have been poorly served by our history teachers. Historian Maury Klein has pondered the confused place of railroad history within the larger bounds of the American story. We have, he says, 'one of the strangest mysteries in our cultural history: the golden age of railroads has come and gone, and we have yet to grasp fully what it meant to American civilization.' Many summary histories of the American story largely ignore railroads and railroad

Dick Kindig found one of the 6500hp 'Big Boys,' the heaviest steam locomotives ever built, exiting Hermosa Tunnel between Laramie and Cheyenne, Wyoming, with an eastbound freight train in April 1950. The locomotive is working at about 10mph, at full throttle.

Regarding railroads, we have been poorly served by our history teachers.

---

people, except for the oft-repeated, nineteenth-century tale of the first transcontinental railroad line and the 'golden spike' (although even that central national episode is often garbled or trivialized).

From any perspective, however, railroads were pivotal to our history for more than one hundred years. They were one of the most important change agents by which our lives have been shaped. Railroads spread immigration through most of North America, became the first 'big business,' became also the unique business that physically interconnected every other economic and social activity in the land, and created some of the greatest wealth –

and some of the greatest economic and human abuses – North America has ever seen. Yet we have trouble grasping these things as vital to the story of who we are as a people. When it comes to railroads, to borrow a fine phrase from George Will, we usually are 'all nostalgia and no history.'

This modest little book certainly does not address most of the issues with which Maury Klein is concerned. The purpose here is quite limited: to make a little more accessible, and a little less mysterious, the railroad heritage of our immediate past. The larger context of railroading's role in helping create our modern industrial economy, however, is also an element behind every one of the pictures in this book.

There were many perspectives on the train from the 1920s through the 1950s. People of color are portrayed here, as employees. Their brothers and sisters used the train throughout this period in the 'Great Migration,' the movement of millions of African Americans from the South to the North – the most important demographic change in the United States in the twentieth century. Said journalist Vernon Jarrett: 'You couldn't do without the train spiritually. It was the vehicle that could take you…away from here.' Despite Jim Crow, rigidly enforced on all the trains in the South and even on some in the Midwest, the railroad played a typically American role for African Americans, as it had done for every migrant group: it took them to new opportunities. What happened after that, of course, was mixed with both triumph and tragedy.

Nearly all of us, of all ethnic backgrounds, have a railroader somewhere in our family trees – a grandparent, an older cousin, some other distant relative. A thought behind this book is to do a little to help rescue the lives of these people from the loving but

In a recent photograph, Joel Jensen captured a moment in evening at the Cheyenne, Wyoming, roundhouse of the Union Pacific Railroad. The locomotive is one of two historic steamers currently run by Steve Lee, Bob Krieger, and other UP employees on special trains.

distorting embrace of the hobbyists. Hobbyists adore the railroad and virtually ignore the railroads' people. Somehow, it is the locomotive and its train that, without human intervention, propel themselves. Endless mechanical details about locomotives and cars are recorded, but there is little attempt to record a detail that actually matters, the people who crew them. In this book, wherever it is possible, you will know their names.

This is the theme, then: the brutal beauty of the steam railroad in its final, 'golden age,' combined with some hint of railroading's all-important human context. It is not a 'romantic' image in any conventional sense of that term. Railroads were built, run, and used by people for very ordinary human reasons. Nostalgia is not enough; worse, it is misleading. Steam railroading is important not because it represents some nostalgic past that, in truth, never was. Steam railroading is important because it was a human tool that radically transformed a continent, affecting everyone.

Great Trains of the Golden Age

'Americans are always moving on. It's an old Spanish custom gone astray, A sort of English fever, I believe, Or just a mere desire to take French leave, I couldn't say. I couldn't really say. But, when the whistle blows, they go away.'
Stephen Vincent Benét, 1943

Americans cannot imagine a world in which they cannot travel freely, without political hindrance. That freedom is rare in the world. But we take it for granted. From the 1870s through the 1940s, if we needed to travel any great distance – for business, for family, for pleasure, for pulling up stakes and moving on – more than likely we took the train. Long before the age of the automobile, the steam locomotive made the United States the most mobile nation on earth. The locomotive was such a potent symbol of our mobility that the journalist Lucius Beebe argued that the locomotive's image was engraved in the imagination of every American. The epitome of this symbolism was the steam locomotive heading up a high-speed, luxury 'limited.' Some trains achieved near-legendary status. *The Twentieth Century Limited* of the New York Central System – connecting the two most important business centers of the US, New York and Chicago – was seriously called 'A National Institution.' Trains in the Far West such as the *Empire Builder*, named for the Great Northern Railway's James J. Hill, allowed Americans to discover a scenic grandeur unknown in the East or South. Farther north, *The Dominion* traversed the rail route that, quite literally, had created the Canadian nation. Few, in fact, could experience this sort of luxury; most of us traveled in the 'day coaches' of the thousands of secondary, unnamed trains. But all of us could dream.

RIGHT: *The Baltimore & Ohio Railroad's elegant train from Jersey City to Washington,* The Royal Blue, *here styled in new art deco streamlining, accelerates away from a station in 1940.*

LEFT: *The* Crescent Limited *of the Southern Railway was the premier train of the South. Running daily between Washington, DC, and New Orleans, its food was among the best on any train in America. Here it pauses on the mainline between Spartanburg and Greenville, South Carolina, about 1929, with new, two-tone green cars.*

BELOW: *The Canadian Pacific's train, the* Trans-Canada Limited, *ran between Montreal and Vancouver via the spectacular Canadian Rockies. En route are the twin Spiral Tunnels, each carved in a loop within opposite mountains. With a 'helper' engine in front and a special open-air car on the rear, this is one train, artfully posed.*

RIGHT: *The New York Central's* Twentieth Century Limited *was doubtless the most celebrated train in North America. Here, one of the 'Hudson' type locomotives designed by Paul Kiefer heads the* Century *on its fast, overnight flight from New York to Chicago, about 1930. Lionel toy trains were modeled on the 'Hudson's' famous face.*

BELOW: *The* Empire Builder *of the Great Northern Railway passes sedately by peaks near Summit, Montana, not far from Marias Pass, leaving a freight train in its wake. The Great Northern billed itself as the 'Gateway to Glacier National Park' and vigorously promoted tourism to the American Northwest.*

LEFT: *One of the great 3460-class passenger locomotives of the Atchison, Topeka & Santa Fe Railway, in 1937. Built for the* Chief, *these engines featured 300-psi boilers and seven-foot-diameter driving wheels.*

RIGHT: *Virtually a trade mark of the Southern Pacific Lines was its oil-burning 'cab-forward' locomotives, usually seen on freight trains. But here, No.4115 approaches Glendale, California, at 40mph with Train 26, the* Owl, *in 1939.*

BELOW: *North of Croton on the Hudson River, a New York Central 'Hudson' type speeds northward with a fast express bound for Albany, while one of many daily local trains works its way south toward New York City.*

ABOVE: *Heavily-used trains sometimes ran in 'sections': one train in the timetable ran as several trains to handle all the passengers. Here, on October 4, 1947, the third section of Santa Fe's* California Limited *takes a sweeping S-curve near Blanchard, New Mexico. The locomotive has its 'stack extension' elevated.*

BELOW: *On many a railroad, the fast mail trains were among the most important on the line. In August, 1940, Union Pacific Train 5, the 18-car* California Fast Mail, *roars out of Cheyenne, Wyoming, behind double-headed locomotive Nos 809 and 823. Mail is in 'head-end' cars at front; passenger cars are to rear.*

RIGHT: *The* Missouri Flyer, *Train 2 of the Burlington Route (the Chicago, Burlington & Quincy), hits 60mph near Keenesburg, Colorado, in 1941. Engine No.3003 is a 'Hudson' type; the New York Central originated and named the type, but many other railroads adopted versions of their own design for fast passenger service.*

LEFT: *Interior of a Pullman sleeping car on the Northern Pacific Railway in the early 1920s. The car is 'made up' here for day use. At night, Pullman attendants 'made down' the car by unfolding the upper berths, converting the seats into lower berths, and hanging privacy curtains.*

BELOW: *Dining aboard has always been one of the pleasures of railroad travel. This is a dining car on the Trans-Canada Limited of the Canadian Pacific, in 1924. While her friends read their menus, the woman at right writes out her meal order, the custom in diners to prevent mistakes in the busy galley.*

RIGHT: *By the 1940s, the interior architecture of passenger cars reflected the 'modern' tastes of the time. The Southern Railway's train, the* Southerner, *featured lounge cars like the* Louisiana. *Also on board were hostesses, 'to welcome passengers' and to help with travelers' problems enroute.*

BELOW: *In 1935, the Milwaukee Road (the Chicago, Milwaukee, St. Paul & Pacific) introduced the sensational, 100mph* Hiawatha, *a 'light-weight' streamlined, steam-hauled train designed to match any of the new diesel streamliners. Patrons lounge in the Hi's Otto Kuhler-styled parlor-observation car at the rear of the train.*

RIGHT: *Once upon a time, railroads were proud of their accomplishments. Every so often, they mounted public exhibitions, such as the Baltimore & Ohio's 'Fair of the Iron Horse' in 1927, the railroad pavilion at Chicago's 'Century of Progress' of 1933, the 'Railroads on Parade' revue at the 1939-40 New York World's Fair, and the Chicago 'Railroad Fair' of 1948-49. After all, 'transportation' and 'railroads' were synonymous terms in the public lexicon, and the public was eager to see new developments that affected their lives so directly. Here are two of the stars of the 1939 New York World's Fair: one of Kiefer's J3 'Hudsons' freshly streamlined for* The Twentieth Century Limited, *and New York Central's ever-famous engine No.999. The* Century *had been completely restyled in the previous year by Henry Dreyfuss. An immediate hit, the revamped* Century *became the subject of press accounts and newsreels seen all over the country, as it cut the time between New York and Chicago to just 16 hours. No.999 had hauled the* Century's *predecessor, the* Empire State Express. *Designed by William Buchanan, No.999 was known to every school kid as the first vehicle of any kind to carry anyone over 100mph, which it did in 1893. Much modified over the years since, No.999 was still operable 46 years later. Both these engines steamed across the stage for World's Fair-goers lucky enough to attend sold-out performances of 'Railroads on Parade.'*

ABOVE: *An art deco sculpture on flashing wheels,* The Twentieth Century Limited *races toward Albany and Chicago in the light of a low, setting sun. Finished in a gun-metal grey, the new, 1938* Century *was restyled inside and out by industrial designer Henry Dreyfuss and garnered an enormous amount of publicity.*

BELOW: *The Baltimore & Ohio's posh* Royal Blue *traverses the 1835 Thomas Viaduct on its way between Washington and Jersey City in the early 1940s. Styled by Otto Kuhler, the new* Royal Blue *competed with other Washington-New York trains; Manhattan passengers connected by dedicated B&O buses to and from Jersey City.*

RIGHT: *The Milwaukee Road topped its 1935* Hiawatha *with a bigger version in 1938, here at Milwaukee's depot. In Kuhler's bold styling of brown, orange, and maroon, the new* Hiawatha *ran daily between Chicago and the Twin Cities (421 miles) in seven hours, at speeds regularly up to 120mph, the fastest in North America.*

RIGHT: *The Reading Railroad fielded a new train in 1937 with stainless-steel cars made by the Budd Co. A round-tailed lounge car ran at each end; thus the train did not need to be turned or reassembled at its Jersey City and Philadelphia end-points for a return journey. Two existing locomotives got stainless cladding and blue-painted driving wheels. Singer Lily Pons christened the train* Crusader *in 1938, after it was named in a public contest.*

LEFT: *No.604 leads the* Pocahontas, *a flagship train of the Norfolk & Western Ry., in 1942. No.604 is a 5500hp 'Northern' type, an advance over the 'Hudsons.' The most powerful 'Northerns' included the Santa Fe and Union Pacific versions shown on p.18; those of the N&W were the most powerful of all.*

BELOW: *One of the grand failures: the Pennsylvania Railroad's one-of-a-kind experimental locomotive No.6100, shown here in Chicago with the PRR train, the* General, *in 1941. Intended to improve on the 'Northern' type, No.6100 had more horsepower than any passenger engine ever. Its styling by Raymond Loewy was showy, but it was too big to handle in terminals.*

RIGHT: *Two passenger engines featured in 'Railroads on Parade' at the 1940 edition of the New York World's Fair: the commemoratively numbered 1940 of the Lackawanna (Delaware, Lackawanna & Western) for its* Phoebe Snow; *and No. 3768, the Pennsylvania Railroad's special locomotive for its top train, the* Broadway Limited, *with streamlined casing by Raymond Loewy.*

BELOW RIGHT: *1938 was a good year for streamlining. Together with* The Twentieth Century, *the* Broadway, *the enlarged* Hiawatha, *and others, the Santa Fe's* Chief *got the treatment. The first of the six 3460-class engines (see p.16) received a blue-and-silver shroud – and the nickname, 'Blue Goose.'*

LEFT: *The Contra Costa was once the largest ferry boat in the world, carrying entire trains of the Southern Pacific across Suisun Bay, between Benicia and Martinez, in northern California. Before a bridge was built in 1930, every 'Overland' and 'Shasta'- route train of the SP had to take the big ferry.*

BELOW: *The Havana Special of the Florida East Coast Railway crosses Long Key Viaduct on its way to Key West, 1932. From right, we see an observation car (with passengers taking the sea air), diner, some Pullman sleepers, several coaches, baggage car, Railway Post Office car, express car, and engine – a lineup typical on many trains.*

RIGHT: *In mountainous territory, passenger trains (as well as freight trains) often needed 'helper' engines on the steepest grades. On a passenger train, the helper always pulled from the front, ahead of the regular locomotive. Coming to a helper district, the passenger train stopped. The helper engine backed from a siding and coupled on. Then transpired one of the best 'shows' in steam railroading: two big engines battling together up the grade. Here, Denver & Rio Grande's* Scenic Limited *blasts from Eagle River Canyon, Colorado, in 1938, with 24 driving wheels on two locomotives pulling hard.*

LEFT: *In this Nicholas Morant photograph, the fireman on helper engine No.5809 leans out to watch the action as three locomotives boost the Canadian Pacific's* Trans-Canada Limited *upgrade near Field, British Columbia, not far from the Spiral Tunnels. At right, a track inspector has wisely set his track car to one side.*

BELOW: *Southern Pacific's* Morning Daylight *crosses the Pajaro River, south of San Francisco, as it speeds to Los Angeles down the 'Coast Route' in the mid-1940s. Californians called the* Daylight *'the most beautiful train in the world,' with its broad orange stripe, flanked above and below in red – the boldest colors on any North American train.*

RIGHT: *The Canadian Pacific Railway's* Dominion *rolls through the gorgeous Bow River Valley west of Banff, Alberta, in Banff National Park in the mid-1940s. The engine is one of the 'Selkirk' type, the CP's largest and named after one of the ranges of the Canadian Rockies crossed by CP. The 'Selkirks' were the last new CP steamers.*

LOCALS AND SHORT LINES

'At all the shows ridicule is the big hit. The minstrel middleman asks the endman, "Where do you get your funny jokes?" Endman replies: "Comparing the running time with the time-table of the Erie Railroad."'

GEORGE JEAN NATHAN, 1910

Commuter trains and branch-line 'locals' were an easy butt of jokes. Modern railroad buffs have forgotten that riding the locals usually wasn't fun; dust sifted from the ventilators, air conditioning was an open window through which cinders rained, and lateness was frequent. The rub was that Americans had become dependent on the train. If you lived outside a larger city, getting to work every day or just getting into town to do a little shopping required the train. The railroad, in fact, along with the trolley, made suburbs possible. If, on the other hand, you lived in a small, rural town you were entirely dependent on the railroad for many of your connections to the wider world – your travel, the goods on your store shelves, your packages and mail, most of your staple food, your big-city newspaper. As the steam railroad spread throughout North America's daunting geography, it carried everything everywhere – up to 90 percent of all intercity passengers and freight at the turn of the twentieth century, still 68 percent of passengers and 75 percent of freight in 1929. The railway was indeed the 'common carrier.' Americans held more hatred than love for the big lines; their monopolistic ways bred deep resentments. The smaller lines were on a more human scale, however, and were rich fodder for the kind of humor found in such popular jokebooks as Thomas W. Jackson's *On a Slow Train through Arkansaw.* The railroaders on these branchlines put up with the japes and insults and went about the business of supporting a growing country.

RIGHT: *In a classic photograph, a Maryland & Pennsylvania RR freight train of one boxcar and a four-wheel 'bobber' (four-wheeled caboose) steams across Gross Trestle, near Sharon, Maryland, in 1955.*

ABOVE: *A quintessential Erie Railroad 'local,' with a coach-baggage 'combination' car and four coaches, in the 1930s. The engine is well painted and polished, probably fresh from overhaul. The light, steel cars are 'Stillwells,' unique to Erie.*

LEFT: *In downtown Salem, Massachusetts ('Witch City'), a 28-year-old locomotive leads a Boston & Maine local train right down a city street, 1937. Crossing watchmen attend. Street running was once common in many US towns.*

RIGHT: *On the mountain-bound Denver & Salt Lake Ry., a short freight train heads east out of Tunnel 26 in South Boulder Canyon, near Pinecliff, Colorado, 1935. No.208 is a little 'Mallet,' with two pairs of cylinders and two sets of driving wheels.*

UPPER LEFT: *The Great Western Sugar Co. of Loveland, Colorado, operated the Great Western Ry. to serve its sugar refinery and other local industries. Here, its little locomotive No.60, built in 1937, has her bell ringing as she pulls into Loveland with a single car of sugar beets, in February, 1941.*

ABOVE: *At the outskirts of Jackson, Mississippi in August, 1940, the engineer has a one-car train easily in hand on the Illinois Central Railroad. On this, the line of Casey Jones, it is humble duty for classic-looking locomotive No.1038, at one time one of the biggest passenger engines for the IC's finest trains. Now, once-proud No.1038 has been bumped down to hauling locals.*

LEFT: *'Ten-Wheeler' No.300 pulls the Denver & Salt Lake Railway's Train 1 over a short trestle west of Rollinsville, Colorado, in May 1940. Two cars make up the train: a Railway Post Office/baggage car and a coach, enough to provide indispensable mail and transportation services to the citizens of the small towns along the D&SL line.*

37

ABOVE: *A few American railroads liked the 'camelback' style locomotive, with cab for the engineer astride the boiler and barely minimal shelter for the fireman between engine and tender. The rationale was a more-forward position for the engineer. The fireman could still stoke the firebox at the back of the boiler… and who cared about the rain, snow, and buffeting wind that assaulted him? One of the last 'camelbacks' speeds a commuter train on the Central Railroad of New Jersey at Bayonne, New Jersey, in March, 1953.*

LEFT: *On the always financially struggling Maryland & Pennsylvania Railroad, a diminutive 'Ma & Pa' steamer hauls a covered-hopper car and a gondola through Woodbrook, Maryland, in 1952, in this Jim Gallagher photo made from the caboose's rear platform.*

ABOVE: *An ancient locomotive of the Northern Pacific Railway ambles down a branchline in Montana in the 1950s, with three boxcars in tow, in a once-typical American scene. The silhouetted caboose (where conductor and brakemen ride) is a 'bay-window' type, without the traditional cupola on the roof.*

RIGHT: *An engineer and a fireman of the Maryland & Pennsylvania RR turn their locomotive on the 'armstrong' turntable at the Falls Road roundhouse, Baltimore, in 1952. The engineer has carefully balanced the engine on the table and set the air brake; the fireman has prepared the fire and set the blower to maintain draft. Now they can rotate their engine and reposition it for a new trip.*

LEFT: *In 1966, six years after the last mainline steamer in regular service in the US went cold, here is decrepit engine No.31 of the Rockton & Rion Railroad, at Rockton, South Carolina. She belches smoke and leaks steam, while pulling a string of hopper cars through a ragged cut near some scraggly pines. Even in the heyday of steam, older engines could soldier on for decades; it was common for a steam locomotive to last forty years or more on duty. Mechanics could renew all the wearing parts – bearings, crankpins, wheel rims, even the firebox; the locomotive's basic structure of boiler, frame, and major castings could last almost indefinitely.*

RIGHT: *The fireman on Kentucky & Tennessee No.10 has swung a water crane around and lowered it into the tender hatch for a fill-up at Stearns, Kentucky, in 1962. Watering is a ritual done every few hours on a steamer. Atop this tender is a 'doghouse' or 'hutch,' in which one of a train's brakemen may ride when underway.*

BELOW: *At east-coast US ports, railroads operated fleets of tug boats, which shuttled barges of railroad cars across the harbors. Here, Brooklyn Eastern District Terminal switcher No.15 – a small, six-wheel 'tank' engine – sorts a string of freight cars, while the tug* Invader *ties up after a stint of work in Upper New York Bay in 1960.*

ABOVE: *In the desert of Arizona near Globe, a freight train of the Magma Arizona Railroad pulls away from a lonely water tank. Such water tanks were once common everywhere in North America.*

LEFT: *At Hoquiam, Washington, in 1963, two small, work-weary 'Mallets' (after Anatole Mallet, inventor of the ancestral type) rest between log- and lumber-hauling duties for the Rayonier Lumber Co. Stack 'bonnets' catch cinders.*

RIGHT: *Near Waterloo, Arkansas, a Reader Railroad freight train backs up, in this scene from 1966. Engine No.1702 is a hand-me-down piece of equipment, bought used from the US Army, but kept spiffy with white-painted driving-wheel rims.*

FREIGHT TRAIN, FREIGHT TRAIN, GOING SO FAST

'They watched it with numb lips and an empty hollowness of fear....
Then the locomotive drew in upon them, loomed enormously above
them...with a terrific drive of...pistoned wheels, all higher than their
heads, a savage furnace-flare of heat, a hard hose-thick hiss of steam.'
THOMAS WOLFE, 1935

Heavy freight has always been the basic work of railroads, generating
the great preponderance of train miles. Throughout the first half of the
twentieth century, railroads hauled the great majority of US and
Canadian freight; railroads were the veins and arteries of the North
American economy. The amounts of cargo borne are staggering. Except
for a severe drop in the Depression-era 1930s, the freight originated on
US railroads averaged 1.3 to 1.5 *billion* tons annually between the mid-
1920s and the mid-1950s. Until the end of World War II, steam
locomotives handled nearly all this massive carriage. Today, one might
wonder how the steamers did it. Compared to the diesels that replaced
them, steamers needed perhaps three to four times more people to run
and maintain them, they had poor adhesion on the rails (they slipped a
lot), and their downtime for service or repairs was two to four times as
much. A voracious fuel consumption was actually the least of their
problems. Yet they were the backbone of rail operations for 120 years
(1830-1950), the period in which our industrial economy reached full
maturity. Skill of the steam-era crew member – engineer, fireman,
conductor, or brakeman – was key; exquisite skill was not simply
desirable, it was the *sine qua non* for the haulage to be done. Glamour
may have gone to the crew on the fast express. Yet it was the crew on the
heavy freight that earned the railroad's keep.

RIGHT: *Hidden in steam, twelve*
driving wheels nearly six feet tall
propel a 'Challenger' - type freighter
of the Western Maryland Railway
up the Alleghenies in 1950.

UPPER LEFT: *One of the all-time best fast-freighters was the 'Texas' type, introduced on the Texas & Pacific in 1925 and then developed on several lines. This is one of the Burlington Route's versions of the breed, managing an over-half-mile-long freight of 59 cars at 40mph near Brush, Colorado, in 1939.*

LOWER LEFT: *In the steam era, the Pennsylvania Railroad was ten percent of all railroading in the US. Over 500 of the I1-type slow-freighters served the Pennsylvania system. I1 No.4595 (with a helper, out of sight) moves a long 'drag' upgrade around the Horseshoe Curve just west of Altoona, Pennsylvania, in 1938.*

UPPER RIGHT: *The 'Northern' type (see p.26) served many railroads in fast freight as well as in passenger duty. These 3000-class 'Northerns' of the Chicago & North Western Railway line up for a publicity photo during World War II. White flags denote 'extra' freights for the surge in war traffic.*

LOWER RIGHT: *Unique to Union Pacific were the massive 9000-class, three-cylinder engines. Between the cylinders at either side in front, another cylinder on the centerline of the engine powered a cranked driving axle. The No.9029 and 38 cars take a curve near Archer, Wyoming, in 1940.*

LEFT: *The grandest 'Texas' - type of all was the 5001-class of the Santa Fe. Each of these 35 nearly-6000hp locomotives could roll freight at 70mph. Here is No.5003 with 70 cars near Vaughn, New Mexico, in 1940.*

BELOW: *'Super-power' was a term coined in the 1920s to denote new locomotive designs with big increases in combustion capacity and hence in power. No.3353 was one of Erie's 105 'Berkshire'-type 'Super-power' engines, here starting up after a stop.*

RIGHT: *A Canadian Pacific freight rockets exhaust skyward as it lifts itself upgrade, near one end of a controlled siding. The Bourgeau Range of the eastern Rockies, Alberta, provides spectacular backdrop. Today's sensibilities abhor the smoke in such a scene – and rightly so. Were steam engines in common use today, we could not tolerate their effluence. We need to forgive yesterday's sensibilities, however. Such smoke, then, had a different meaning: wages being earned.*

UPPER LEFT: *Yes, freight engines pulled passenger trains. In this scene from the 1930s, two 'Selkirk'-type freighters (see also p.31) are 'double-headed' on a Canadian Pacific passenger train, preparing to climb the Rockies.*

LOWER LEFT: *Even in gentler terrain, older and smaller locomotives often had to 'double head' to handle the freight. On New York Central subsidiary Ulster & Delaware, two engines lead boxcars across a country lane. The 800's whistle blows and bell swings.*

ABOVE: *Helpers galore. Five Southern Pacific locomotives assault the 'horseshoe' near San Luis Obispo, California, headed for the summit of the Santa Lucia grade. Train's end is visible at left; iced 'reefers' are full of fruit and vegetables.*

RIGHT: *Two well-matched 'Mountain'-type engines of the Denver & Rio Grande Western carry a northbound freight of 66 cars near Pikeview, Colorado, in August 1941. The Rio Grande was one of several western lines that painted engine fronts and fireboxes silver.*

LEFT: *On the Southern Railway in the late 1940s, a freight passes the station and water tank at Leeds, Alabama. Note white waiting room, arrival-and-departure board, and signs for Western Union and Railway Express. Engine is an Ls-2.*

ABOVE: *In a scene once typical all over America, a freight bustles into an unidentified town. The railroad was lifeline. Against a wooded skyline, an Illinois Central train of the late 1930s pulls across three underpasses and into the yard.*

RIGHT: *Long Island Rail Road tugs and barges handle cars laden with coal, lumber, oil, and manufactures at Long Island City, while the towers of Manhattan rise up in the background. The water is ice-covered; it is February 1945.*

LEFT: *On the Baltimore & Ohio, a freight comes downgrade over Tray Run Viaduct in 1949. There is some brakeshoe smoke back in the train; a trail of steam comes from the engine's electric dynamo. No.7609 is a huge, four-cylinder EM-1, among the most powerful steam locomotives anywhere.*

RIGHT: *At Castle Gate, Utah, on the Price River, the canyon echoes to the wondrous thunder of a heavy coal train's two straining helpers. It is December 1951 on the Denver & Rio Grande Western; the coal is going west, toward Salt Lake. No.1405 has devices called 'overfire jets' installed along the firebox (between the rear driving wheel and the cab); these were designed to help reduce smoke – but not too successfully today.*

LEFT: *In the Congress Street Yards of the Illinois Central on Chicago's lakefront, several types of IC locomotives are arrayed for a publicity picture in 1952. The wires overhead are for electric-powered commuter trains. These Iowa-Division steamers, not needing the wires, are scheduled to depart westbound with general freight and dressed meat.*

LEFT: *In a splendid picture by Dick Kindig, two of Union Pacific's magnificent, four-cylinder 'Challengers' storm Sherman Hill at 40mph, west of Cheyenne, Wyoming, on a cold May 17, 1953.*

ABOVE: *In the steam age, an essential part of fresh-food shipping was the well-iced refrigerator car. Men of the Seaboard Air Line Railroad guide the ice blocks into their proper bunkers at an icing station.*

BELOW: *In the fall of 1961, photographer John Gruber caught a kid in the time-honored act of 'counting the cars.' The cars are full of sugar beets; this is the Hurrich beet station on the Great Western Ry. in Colorado.*

BACKWOODS AND NARROW GAUGE

*'With us a locomotive steam-engine is still, as it were, a beast of prey –
But there, in the Western States, it has been taken to the bosoms of them
all as a domestic animal; no one fears it, and the little children run
about almost among its wheels.'*
ANTHONY TROLLOPE, 1862

Backwoods lines could be standard gauge like the large railroads (4 feet, 8½ inches, measured from the inside of one rail to the inside of the other) or narrow (usually 3 feet in the US). Most of these remote carriers were standard gauge, but surely the most celebrated were the 'three-footers,' such as the Denver & Rio Grande Western's narrow-gauge system in the high country of Colorado and northern New Mexico (not to be confused with the Rio Grande's much more extensive standard system) and the East Broad Top Railroad in the soft-coal region of southwestern Pennsylvania. These lines provided all the services of a larger carrier, accommodating passengers and freight, and became familiar, everyday servants to the small communities they interconnected. The choice of three-foot gauge was touted by some promoters in the nineteenth and early twentieth centuries as being economic: in building such lines, excavations could be narrower and ties could be shorter; in running the line, the smaller locomotives and cars would be cheaper. The savings proved chimerical. More specialized were the logging lines, used to haul timber from forest to mill. Owned by lumber companies east and west, such deepwoods railways came in standard or narrow gauge. A logging line's hairpin curves and stiff grades required a special form of locomotive to give great pull at slow speed: the 'Shay,' 'Heisler,' and 'Climax' types. In the steam era, these were the most humble of 'domestic animals.'

RIGHT: *Hillcrest Lumber Co. No.10,
at Mesatchie Lake, Vancouver
Island, British Columbia, 1960.
No.10 is a 'Climax' type that
hauled lumber to Nanaimo for
transshipment to the mainland.*

LEFT: *In the wooded foothills of the Sierra Nevada Mountains of California, West Side Lumber Co. No.15, a 'Shay,' drifts downhill with a train of logs in 1958. The 'Shay' has three vertical cylinders, turning a gearshaft to power the wheels.*

ABOVE: *The three-foot-gauge East Broad Top Railroad was originally built to tap the coal of East Broad Top Mountain in southwestern Pennsylvania. The EBT became, as well, all-purpose transportation for the towns on its route. A remnant runs today, for tourists.*

RIGHT: *East Broad Top steamer No.14 blows steam from its cylinders, as it rolls off the turntable at the roundhouse at Rockhill Furnace, Pennsylvania.*

UPPER LEFT: *In February 1961, Alan Steinheimer and his dog, Shadow, take a snowshoe hike east of Chama, New Mexico. A Denver & Rio Grande Western three-foot-gauge freight steams by, heading for a 10,000-foot summit and the town of Cumbres.*

LOWER LEFT: *In the 1930s on the Rio Grande narrow gauge in Colorado, an 'express' comes downhill. The engine's snowplow-pilot is designed for high-mountain winter storms, but this is summer, and a canvas water bag dangles off the tender's side.*

RIGHT: *As does the East Broad Top, the Rio Grande narrow gauge still runs today in part, for tourists. A portion now called the Durango & Silverton operates from Durango, Colorado. Old mountain-climber 488 rests in the Durango shop.*

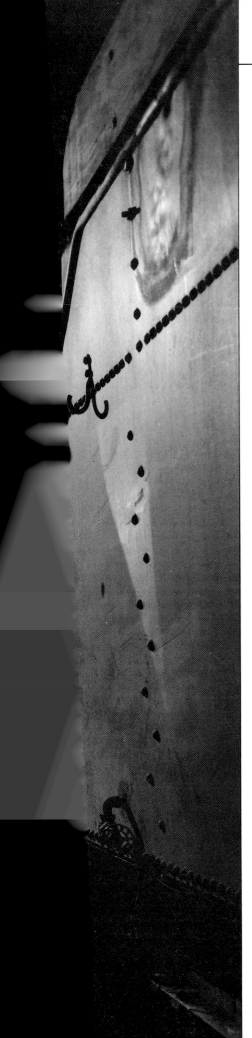

LEFT: *In the old roundhouse at Alamosa, Colorado, Denver & Rio Grande narrow-gauge engines 492 and 483 slumber quietly on a winter's evening in 1961, warmed by steam from the railroad shops' central steam plant.*

BELOW: *In this Farm Security Administration photograph from the mid-1930s, sheepmen load lambs aboard a narrow-gauge livestock car on the Rio Grande at Cimarron, Colorado.*

ABOVE: *This is the standard-gauge Sierra Railroad; engine No.28 shifts a car of wood chips in the yard at Jamestown, California, in 1949, sandwiched between the yard's water tank and an old Rock Island Lines boxcar.*

LEFT: *Two Rio Grande narrow-gauge engines wrestle snow-fighting equipment up the line. The train is about to plunge into a tunnel near Toltec, New Mexico, in this January 1963 photo by Ron Ziel, taken on-board.*

RIGHT: *The locomotive may not be leaning quite so precariously as the picture suggests, but this dramatic view from the fireman's cab-window hints at the always parlous state of the Rio Grande's high-country, slim-gauge system.*

DOWN BY THE STATION

'It will set the whole world a-gadding. Grave, plodding citizens will be flying about like comets.... All local attachments will be at an end.'

LETTER TO AN INDIANA NEWSPAPER, 1830

It is hard, today, to understand the social significance of the railroad station in its time. Today, we escape the city in our own car on a dozen different highways, or we take the plane, or – rarely – we take the bus or train. Every boundary of the city is as permeable as gauze. It was not always so. Before the steam age, most people didn't travel very much; hence the various wagon roads out of town also sufficed for stagecoach, horseback, or 'shank's mare.' Steam power produced, by far, the most radical alterations in human mobility ever experienced. Not even the airplane's dramatic impact can compare. From the beginning of recorded time, distance and speed – and thus human interchange – were limited by wind or muscle. With steam, travel became a norm rather than a rarity. And, inland, all of it was mediated by the railway station. Before long, the railway station became *the* gateway, the great door to the world beyond one's own. In smaller towns, the station may have been a rather undistinguished building. But it was the town's portal. For one's own departure on any sort of travel, for the coming of faraway friends and relatives, for mail, for the sending and receipt of every kind of express shipment – the station was the portal. In cities, the stations became grandiose, to reflect their importance; 'temples of transportation' became a hackneyed phrase. Yet somehow they were always human in architecture, evoking continuity with the past. Wondrous gateways they were.

RIGHT: *Point of Rocks Junction, Maryland, on the 'mother of American railroads,' the Baltimore & Ohio. A freight steams westward; the track at right comes from Washington, DC; 'KG' Tower stands guard.*

ABOVE: *'At the platform…' It is morning, and a commuter train arrives at South Station, Boston, 1937. The compact engine, of the Boston & Albany, is an uncommon type designed and built nine years before, just for commuter service.*

BELOW: *Omaha station, Nebraska, April 1942. A soldier shipping overseas awaits a troop train; he passes a few minutes regarding a Chicago & North Western streamlined 'Hudson' and its train, which prepares for departure.*

RIGHT: *Everyday life in America in the peacetime year of 1948, in this wonderful Phil Hastings picture. At Bradford, Vermont, on the Boston & Maine, mail sacks, express boxes, travelers – and pre-teen boys – are ready for 'the southbound.'*

RIGHT: *The big-city station was once the place to show off the latest railroad 'high tech' to an admiring public. Here, inside Windsor Station, Montreal, in 1931, the Canadian Pacific exhibits its experimental, multi-pressure locomotive No.8000.*

LEFT: *Behind the scenes, many worked to keep the trains moving in the steam era. This ticket agent checks his inventory. Above him are ranks of pre-printed tickets for over a hundred destinations; at hand, various transportation forms; below, passenger timetables.*

BELOW: *Well-kept flower beds and shrubs typify a Canadian station. At Merrickville, Ontario, the stationmaster and family live on the second floor, a familiar practice in Canada and the US. Here, a polished engine and train have arrived; a railroad official (left), engineer, and conductor confer.*

RIGHT: *Some otherwise humble stations served definitely 'upscale' destinations. This is the modest platform at White Sulphur Springs, West Virginia, serving the tony 'Greenbrier' resort. The Chesapeake & Ohio Railway's* train George Washington *pauses. (The engine carries on its front its two air pumps for the train brake system, a C&O practice.)*

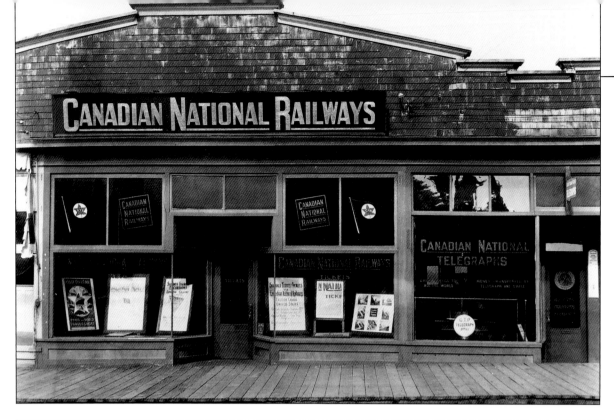

LEFT: *Downtown ticket offices were maintained by railroads in many cities and towns. This is the Canadian National Railways' ticket sales office in Prince Rupert, British Columbia, in the 1920s. Tour posters face the wooden sidewalk.*

BELOW: *Trackside at Union Depot, Stillwater, Minnesota, in September 1926. 'Union' meant that two or more railroads cooperated in the station's operation: in this case the Burlington, the Chicago & North Western, and the Milwaukee Road. This depot is from 1885.*

RIGHT: *Many stations, even small ones, were architectural gems. On the Southern Ry., 'carpenter gothic' trim festoons the little station and waiting shed at Ladson, South Carolina, shown in the 1920s. The signal on the mast is the 'train order board.'*

LOWER RIGHT: *Conductors check watches and 'log in' at a Union Pacific station. Railroads unilaterally imposed the system of 'Standard Time' on the US in 1883, and railroads brought a sense of precision in time unknown before. In this 1940s shot, posters promote war bonds.*

LEFT: *Crowds of travelers fill 'the greatest station of them all,' Pennsylvania Station, New York City. In 1945, its record year, 109 million passengers arrived or departed its gates. Nearly as many passed through in 1946, when this photo was made. Planned under Alexander Cassatt – Pennsylvania Railroad president and probably the most visionary leader ever in American railroading – the building opened in 1910.*

LEFT: *Pennsylvania Station occupied a full city block, on seven and a half acres of land. Its Main Waiting Room – seen at the center of the picture – was 110 feet wide and 300 feet long, and had a coffered ceiling 150 feet high. The Train Concourse, with its glass domes, was one of the largest enclosed public spaces in North America. Surrounding it all were Roman columns, arranged in facades known to every New Yorker.*

RIGHT: *A view of a part of the Train Concourse, Pennsylvania Station. In addition to the long-distance and commuting passengers, many came to Penn Station to greet or see off travelers, or to dine at its restaurants. Total visitation was a half-million people per day. Over 850 trains a day entered or departed through two tunnels under the Hudson River and four tunnels under the East River. Trains ran with electric locomotives in the tunnels; steam engines handled trains beyond relay points. 'Manhattan Transfer' in New Jersey was the locomotive relay point south of the Hudson. In 1946, the year of this picture, trains included the* Broadway Limited *(arch-rival of the New York Central's* Twentieth Century Limited *which ran from Grand Central Terminal) and the* Trail Blazer *to Chicago, the* Spirit of St Louis *and the* Jeffersonian *to St Louis, the* Congressional, *the* Senator, *and the* Federal *to Washington, scores of trains to Long Island, and numerous other trains north to Boston and Montreal, as well as south as far as Miami and New Orleans.*

LEFT AND BELOW: *Medium-size stations, too, were showpiece landmarks for their cities. The Atlanta Terminal Station (seen also on pp.92-93) opened in 1910, the same year Penn Station in New York was completed. Rather than Roman-inspired architecture, the Atlanta station took a* beaux arts *look. The intent was the same: to convey via grand architectural design the social and economic power of the railroad.*

ABOVE AND RIGHT: *The station as gateway. In the obviously posed shot above, passengers make ready to board Train 42, the* Chesapeake & Ohio's George Washington, *at Richmond, Virginia. Who could be so completely cheerful in the war year of 1943? Would the three servicemen return from war alive? What kind of world awaited the youngsters? What sort of future did the Redcap face, as he stands apart? Yet all knew the significance of the human journeys here; life would be changed inevitably by one's passing through this gate. At right, it is now 1946 in North Station, Boston. War is done, and a long dreamed-of respite beckons at 'winter's playgrounds.' A gateway is indifferent; the traveler never is.*

RAILROAD SHOPS AND ENGINE TERMINALS

'Detached engines hurried in and out of sheds and roundhouses, seeking their trains…trundling up and down, clanking, shrieking, their bells filling the air with the clangour of tocsins.'
FRANK NORRIS, 1902

The steam locomotive was a labor-intensive beast. It required a small army to keep it fueled, watered, serviced, repaired and, every few years, overhauled. Every railroad in the steam era maintained a network of engine servicing terminals, most of these no more than 100 miles apart from each other, since that was usually the maximum distance a steam locomotive could work on the road before it needed fuel, lubrication, sand replenished, ashes dumped, and, very often, minor repairs. Operationally, railroads therefore were divided into 'divisions' of about 100 miles in length, each under a superintendent. A major yard and an engine terminal were fixtures of those cities which were 'division points.' The working characteristics of the steam locomotive hence determined much of a railroad's organization and geography. The most demanding and exacting labor occurred in the vast 'backshops,' of which any major railroad had at least one, where the heaviest repairs and rebuilding for locomotives were centralized. People here made their own 'spare parts.' Highly skilled machinists, mechanics, foundrymen, boilermakers, steam fitters, layout men, valve-setters, air-brake specialists, and others could make any repair, renew any part, or indeed manufacture an entire, brand-new locomotive – slicing, bending, riveting, and welding the thick sheet steel, making the patterns, pouring the castings, machining the parts, and precisely assembling the whole.

RIGHT: *Shaffers Crossing engine terminal of the Norfolk & Western Railway, in Roanoke, Virginia, 1943. Roundhouse in background; unique 'run-through' lubrication sheds at left and right.*

LEFT: *The managers have asked the employees to stand away from the camera, so we cannot see the activity in this, one of several great halls at Canadian Pacific's Angus Shops near Montreal. Such huge 'backshops' were essential to steam railroading. At Angus, locomotives were repaired – and built new from scratch.*

RIGHT: *A young, skilled machinist at Angus poses with a milling machine, used to make precision parts. He adjusts the machine's dividing head to set the cut; his apron is stained by cutting oil. His machine, like that of his colleague, is driven by a belt from an overhead shaft.*

LOWER RIGHT: *An all-woman crew cleans locomotives at the Southern Pacific roundhouse in Oakland, California, during World War II. In spring 1945, near war's end, the number of women working on American railroads peaked at 115,000, in nearly all occupations – almost 10 percent of the work force.*

ABOVE: *An 800-class, high-speed passenger locomotive of the Union Pacific Railroad takes on coal at the Council Bluffs, Iowa, engine terminal in 1939.*

BELOW: *Cloquet, Minnesota, 1935 – Superintendent Jensen of the Duluth & Northeastern Ry. gives his engine crew instructions for a trip to Tall Timbers.*

RIGHT: *A locomotive shop foundry crew beats white-hot steel into shape under the steam hammer for a new side rod, in this scene from the 1930s.*

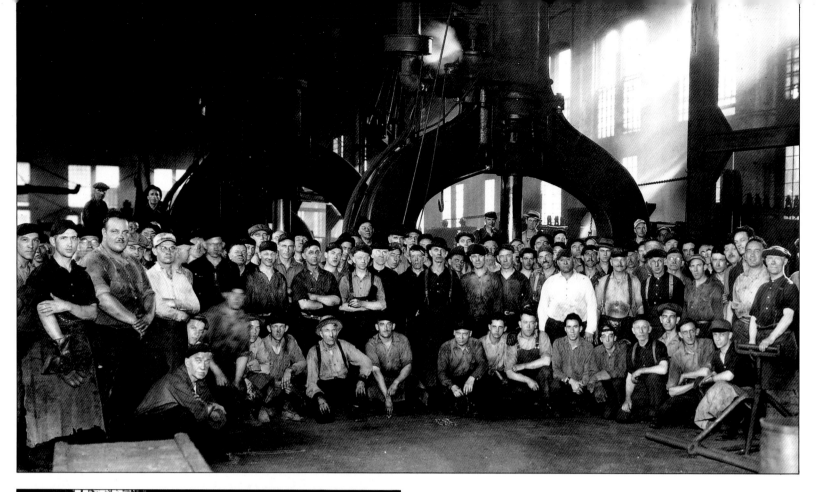

ABOVE: *Foundrymen stand in the Juniata Shops of the Pennsylvania Railroad, Altoona, Pennsylvania, in the 1940s. At Altoona, crews like these maintained the largest fleet of steam locomotives run by any railroad in North America. And, over the years, they built nearly 7000 locomotives of the Pennsy's own design.*

RIGHT: *On Minnesota's Duluth & Northeastern, a repaired locomotive maneuvers at the shop and roundhouse at Cloquet. A brakeman rides on the tender's rear step, in order to throw switches along the engine's path. Backlit by the sun, the cloud from the stack is clean steam, condensing on a cold January day. Though the scene is timeless, the little engine is nearing the end of the line; it is 1962, and final retirement is soon to come.*

LEFT: *Mechanics of the Central Vermont Railway remove the front of a locomotive, at the shop at St Albans, Vermont. One man cuts a troublesome nut and stud with his acetylene torch, while his partner stands by to knock the connection free with his sledge. The engine is in the shop for a complete overhaul.*

LEFT: *The most powerful steam locomotive ever built in series production was the 'Allegheny' type. Designed and constructed by the Lima Locomotive Works, Lima, Ohio, for the Chesapeake & Ohio Ry., some were also used on the Virginian Ry. On test, they registered nearly 7500hp at the drawbar, 1000 more than the legendary 'Big Boys' of the Union Pacific. Here, 'Allegheny' No.1622 rolls off the turntable at the C&O roundhouse in Huntington, West Virginia, while sister No.1627 stands by; a third 1600 is in the foreground with only its fully-coaled tender in view. Two supervisors – their hats informally distinguishing their rank – watch the running gear of No.1622 as it moves regally by.*

RIGHT: *Roundhouses came in all sizes. This mini-edition is the former Buffalo, Rochester & Pittsburgh roundhouse at Butler, Pennsylvania. Extra car wheels stand in rows on either side; an old B&O freighter rides the table.*

LOWER RIGHT: *On the Denver & Rio Grande Western narrow-gauge, a brakeman walks back from his caboose during a switching move in the yard at Chama, New Mexico, about 1950.*

BELOW: *Alda Durling operates the big turntable at the Southern Pacific roundhouse at Dunsmuir, California, in November 1942. During the war, women worked in dozens of trades on nearly every US railroad.*

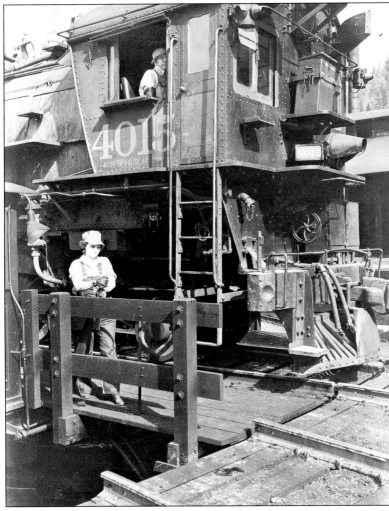

UPPER LEFT: *At the Brooklyn Eastern District Terminal engine shed in the fall of 1963, four switching locomotives stand, while a new diesel pulls cars. The steamers are 'tank engines' (i.e., sans tenders, with their water and fuel in on-board 'tanks' or bunkers); these four will soon be retired.*

LOWER LEFT: *Jim Shaughnessy caught heavy steamers being watered at the Turcot Yard of Canadian National Railways in Montreal, on a frigid January day in 1954. No.6308 has an 'all-weather' cab having better protection for engine crews in the harsh Canadian climate. A crewman braves the chill.*

RIGHT: *In this Ed Nowak photo, the fireman wipes down the light-weight, roller-bearing side rods of a new, high-wheeled passenger locomotive on the New York Central in the 1940s. The engine is one of the 'highest-tech' steamers, NYC's 5000hp 'Niagara' type (a variation of the 'Northern'). Designed by innovative mechanical engineers Paul Kiefer of the NYC and Alfred Bruce of the American Locomotive Co., the 'Niagaras' pulled* The Twentieth Century Limited *and other trains. These engines set all-time records for steam efficiency in everyday use and held off diesels for a time.*

IN THE
LAST DAYS

'What's gone and what's past help should be past grief.'
<small>SHAKESPEARE, *THE WINTER'S TALE*: ACT III, SCENE 2</small>

The last American steam locomotives from the three major builders – the Baldwin Locomotive Works of Philadelphia, the American Locomotive Co. of Schenectady, New York, and the Lima Locomotive Works of Lima, Ohio – left their factories in 1948 and 1949. In 1944, 40,000 steamers served US railroads in frontline duty; by 1960, the last one in regular service on a major American carrier dropped its fire. The large Canadian lines sidetracked their steamers by 1962. There was grief. Buffs felt it was all a malicious plot by heartless railway managers. The buffs' grief was misdirected and ignorant; in the changed postwar world, the high costs attendant to steam threatened to help sink the entire railroad enterprise. The real grief came to the legions of men and women dependent on steam for their livelihoods. Between 1946 and 1962, employment on the big US carriers fell from 1.4 million to 700,000 – a cut in half – largely due to the efficiencies brought by diesels on the road, at the servicing terminals, and in the backshops. The Canadian lines endured relatively similar trauma. Every city and town with a railroad terminal or shop was affected, and there were several thousand such communities. No more sweeping industrial change has occurred in North America. Today, US railroads are producing more ton-miles than ever: over 1.1 *trillion* freight ton-miles in 1993, almost double the records set during the frenetic years of World War II. We stand, however, on the shoulders of those who came before us.

<small>RIGHT: *In the mid-1940s, two trains ready to depart Atlanta's Terminal Station: an Atlanta-Washington train behind Ps-4 class steamer No.1393, and the* Crescent *behind new E6 class diesels.*</small>

LEFT: *At Los Angeles about 1940, hostler Beal, responsible for engine servicing, fills the sand dome of Santa Fe locomotive No.3437, a passenger steamer. A harbinger of change, a General Motors-built E2 diesel from the Super Chief growls past. Santa Fe was one of the first major carriers fully to endorse diesels; steam last ran on AT&SF in the summer of 1957.*

LOWER LEFT: *In Alburg, Vermont, a Rutland Railroad crew has finished a run in January 1949. In the enginehouse, the conductor 'logs out'; the engineer cleans up. Their train will soon be discontinued, as Rutland feels the pinch of postwar traffic declines. Ultimately, the railroad will be abandoned.*

RIGHT: *In this close-up by Glenn Beier, the weary face of a Southern Pacific steamer is streaked by the residue of fuel-oil smoke. It is 1956 at the San Jose, California, yards. No.4354, once one of SP's finest passenger engines, serves out her last months in San Jose-San Francisco commuter duty.*

LEFT: *On the east side of California's San Joaquin Valley in 1955, Sierra Railroad No.38 pulls a short freight train near Cooperstown, headed for Oakdale. The crew has eased off throttle and fuel, clearing the stack, and steam lifts from the boiler's safety valves.*

LOWER LEFT: *On a frosty day in the mid-1950s, double-headed locomotives start up a heavy freight at Lenoxville, Quebec, near Sherbrooke. The heavy black smoke shows that the two engines are working hard; the condensing white steam betrays the near-zero temperature.*

RIGHT: *A Canadian National passenger train prepares for a night departure in the late 1950s. Major Canadian railroads kept steam a few years longer than did US carriers. While diesels increased in number, steam continued on mainlines in Canada until the early 1960s.*

BELOW: *One of the US hold-outs against the diesel revolution was the Louisville & Nashville Railroad. Under the coal tower at DeCoursey, Kentucky, two M-l class engines ('Big Emmas') wait to refuel in 1956. Dependent on coal for much of its revenue, L&N bought new M-ls until 1949.*

LEFT: *In a Richard Steinheimer photograph, a Southern Pacific night freight pulls slowly out of the West Oakland, California, yards near San Francisco Bay, bound for Tracy. It is 1956 – the last year of regular SP steam runs. Said the photographer, 'the rising steam exhausts – each one blown by the cold, damp wind off the Bay – seemed almost like farewell waves....'*

RIGHT: *In the mid-1950s, a Southern Pacific cab-forward locomotive backs down in the West Oakland, California, yard to pick up a freight train for Roseville. The fireman watches to the rear. To raise boiler pressure for the work ahead, he has slightly increased the flow of fuel-oil to his fire, darkening the exhaust. His skills will soon be obsolete.*

LEFT: *The mighty fall. At Erwin, Tennessee, in 1962, a line of Clinchfield Railroad locomotives are left for scrap. Already, a piece of another scrapped engine's boiler has been tossed casually atop the 661's tender. These are 'Challenger'-type locomotives (see pp.44 and 56), once the newest and most powerful on the Clinchfield.*

RIGHT: *In the last months of their steam operations, larger railroads in the US and Canada staged commemorative excursions and 'last runs.' Here, on October 14, 1962, the Canadian National Railway runs a special train from Quebec City with 'Pacific'-type No.5107 and 'Northern'-type No.6153 doing the honors. Rail buffs lean out of the second baggage car to take pictures.*

LEFT: *Burlington locomotive No.6316 meets its fate in June 1962 at the Northwestern Steel & Wire Co. scrapyard in Sterling, Illinois. The cutting man, with acetylene torch, has taken off the whole top half of the boiler shell, which a crane is lifting away.*

RIGHT: *At the Sanford, North Carolina, shop of the 3.4-mile-long Atlantic & Western Ry. in 1962, old steam locomotive No.1 stands derelict. Rusting with No.1 is a rail bus, once A&W's passenger service. Weeds fill the turntable pit.*

THE RAILROADERS

'One machine can do the work of fifty ordinary men. No machine can do the work of one extraordinary man.'

ELBERT HUBBARD, 1910

Anyone knows, who has had the privilege of meeting many of them: 'old school' railroaders displayed a quiet but intense pride of craft. In the steam era they were 'an aristocracy of labor,' in the words of one historian. Visible to the public everyday in every city and town, railroaders performed tasks on which community welfare and safety critically depended. Hence they commanded good pay and high respect. Whether or not an employee 'liked' or cared much about steam engines (and few did), the craft of railroading – in the engine cabs, on the 'rear-end' freight crews, in the passenger cars, on the track gangs, in the towers, in the shops, in the stations – demanded a degree of professionalism greater than in most industrial work. The key was the farflung, decentralized nature of railroading. Train and engine crews, dispatchers, towermen, traffic agents, track inspectors, signal repairmen, and many other trades worked well away from direct supervision. Their work was highly complex, far from repetitive, and demanded judgment and self reliance. Such decentralized responsibility was also true of machinists and blacksmiths in the repair shops, of mechanics in the maintenance sheds, and of crews on the track. Some modern social historians, with no personal experience of industrial life, and focusing too much on a narrow range of factory work, miss an essential human quality of any skilled work – its pride. Railroaders knew it well.

RIGHT: *Near Gaviota, California, on the Southern Pacific 'Coast Route' north of Santa Barbara, a Mexican American track foreman and crew repair a spur switch in the early 1950s.*

LEFT: *In 1943, two women stack empty drums that will soon be loaded with lubricating oil for the European front. An Erie 'Berkshire' rolls by, in a wartime scene in western New York State.*

TOP, LEFT AND RIGHT: *The tower operator was crucial in railroad movements. At left is operator Bunker in 'PD' Tower at Patchogue, New York, on the Long Island RR in 1925. At right is a tower on the Union Pacific at Omaha, 1954.*

RIGHT: *Railroad operators often worked in lonely outposts, receiving train orders by wire and relaying these as written 'Form 19' orders to crews. A dog could be good company at night.*

LEFT: *The conductor is 'captain' on any train; engineer and other crew members report to the conductor. On the Louisville & Nashville in 1957, a passenger conductor accounts for tickets. His 'office' is an empty coach seat (with a head-rest linen that has been put on backward).*

BELOW: *The conductor is also the road boss on freight trains, and the caboose was his office in railroading's traditional era. A freight conductor stands in the doorway of a new Union Pacific caboose in the late 1950s; in his hand is the train crew member's most basic tool, a signal lantern.*

RIGHT: *'Telling stories' in a Pullman car in the early 1930s. Porters organized the Brotherhood of Sleeping Car Porters in 1925, with A. Philip Randolph as first president. Randolph fought for better working conditions; a porter often worked 400 hours per month.*

BELOW, LEFT AND RIGHT: *Trackmen tighten bolts at rail joints in early spring, 1953, on the Chicago & North Western west of Lusk, Wyoming. Baggagemen load some bedraggled-looking boxes on the Louisville & Nashville, while the impatient conductor regards his watch.*

LEFT: *In time-honored ritual before departure, the conductor hands up a copy of a 'Form 19' train order – which specifies operating clearance for the track ahead and sets out instructions for meeting points with opposing trains – while he and the engineer check the accuracy of their watches. By its characteristic stem, one can see that the conductor's watch is a Hamilton, the most desired railroader's precision timepiece. Through the cab window can be seen the locomotive's pendant throttle – ready to unleash 5000 horsepower.*

RIGHT: *At the Radnor yard in Nashville, Tennessee, in the 1940s, a hostler fills a thirsty tender on a Louisville & Nashville freight locomotive. His right hand controls the water flow; his foot holds down the spout against recoil from the water's torrent.*

BELOW: *His left arm up so as to adjust the throttle, the engineer of Sierra Railroad's well-maintained oil-burner No.28 has her on the gallop near Keystone, California, in July, 1958. White flags by the headlight show it's an 'extra' train, not on the regular schedule.*

LEFT: *A hostler on the Mississippian Railway fills his engine's oil cups at Fulton, Mississippi in April, 1966.*

BELOW LEFT: *Engineer Kundrick takes a break at Brownville, Alabama, on the 11-mile Mobile & Gulf RR in March, 1966.*

RIGHT: *Before the era of mobile radios, crew members on moving trains got their train orders 'on the fly' as this freight conductor on the Western Maryland Ry. is doing in this Frank Quin photo made at Deal, Pennsylvania in 1940. The train's engineer has already picked up his copy from the order hoop. Another engine waits in the siding; a young lad watches from his bike.*

LEFT: *A work crew replaces a drive shaft while a welder, at front, repairs a brake beam on an ancient 'Shay' locomotive at Kellerman, Alabama. Photographer Ron Ziel found these labors underway at the Twin Seams Mining Co. after a derailment in 1962.*

RIGHT: *A fireman stokes engine No.14 on the East Broad Top Railroad, in this picture by Smithsonian photographer Jeff Tinsley. The fireman's job was highly skilled. He had to place his 'shots' of coal on the roaring fire with great accuracy so as to maintain an even firebed, all the while responding to the locomotive's ever-changing power demands. He also regulated the water supply to the boiler, varying water rate and firing, together, to keep the desired steam pressure. Mechanical ability was required, to handle problems enroute. Years were needed to hone these fine skills.*

LEFT: *Fireman Arkinstall, a veteran of steam passenger-train service on the Pennsylvania RR, uses a firehook to help prepare the coal firebed on former Great Western Ry. engine No.60 for later departure. Above the open firedoor is a rack for oil cans.*

BELOW: *The crew of Rockton & Rion Ry. engine No.1 discuss the next part of their day's work at Anderson Quarry, South Carolina, in March, 1966. No.1's cab roof shows battering from years of impacts from the loader used to fill the engine's coal bunker.*

RIGHT: *Track construction crew members line up for lunch at a Western Pacific camp train's kitchen car at Milpitas, California, north of San Jose in the early 1950s. The men are building yard tracks for a new Ford Motor Co. auto assembly plant.*

BELOW: *Shopmen proudly pose on a 'Northern'-type locomotive they have overhauled at the Chicago & North Western heavy repair facility in Chicago in the late 1930s. Peak rail employment in the twentieth century was nearly two million, with ten times that number in rail-dependent jobs.*

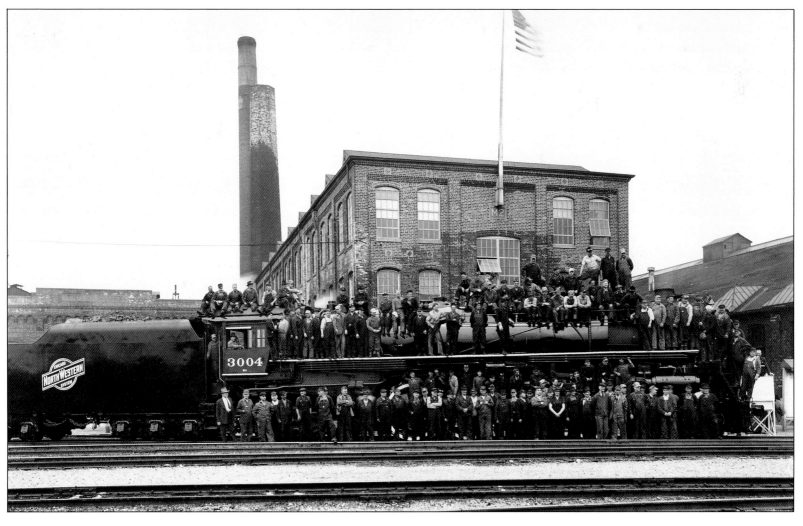

PRESERVED
STEAM

*'It is more than a machine, it is almost a living being; ... it breathes;
the steam which issues at regular periods from the pipes, and
is condensed into a white cloud, resembles the quick breathing
of a racehorse.'*
MICHEL CHEVALIER, 1839

Museums stuff and mount things. That is one kind of preservation.
The specimen, whether fish or locomotive, is set aside for posterity. The
museum provides interpretation – perhaps a sign, or in better-funded
institutions, an interactive video to help the visitor better understand the
specimen and its meaning. Still and all, it is 'history under glass.' Without
such preservation, much of our cultural heritage would disappear, of
course. But especially for the interpretation of our industrial history, the
special challenge is to try to make it real on its own terms – to bring
something of the experience of industrial work out from under the glass.
The steam locomotive is certainly one of those industrial artifacts for
which there is simply no comparison between a stuffed one and a live
one. A few hundred operable steam locomotives are now left around the
world, preserved mostly by buffs or tourist train operators with no
thought of 'historical interpretation.' Without fully appreciating it,
however, these operators preserve something else: the deep knowledge
and human, hands-on skills that are the steam arts. More precious than
any machine, *this knowledge and skill* are the treasures, the historical
legacy of two centuries. Historians understand the wider contexts,
perhaps, but they often understand little of working lives. Steam
practitioners and historians need to get together – for the benefit of both,
and for the better public understanding of our industrial heritage.

RIGHT: *Steamtown National
Historic Site in Scranton,
Pennsylvania, with 'big steam' on
duty. At left, a Canadian National
heavy freight engine; at right, a
Baldwin six-wheel switcher.*

LEFT: *At the Steamtown National Historic Site in Scranton, Pa., roundhouse foreman Roger Samuels uses a hose to clean out the ashpan of Canadian Pacific No.2317, a heavy passenger locomotive.*

RIGHT: *Samuels is completing a repair to an electrical junction box at the front of No.2317 that connects to the locomotive's headlight. No.26, formerly a shop switcher for the Baldwin Locomotive Works, awaits service.*

BELOW: *Readying for departure, the engine crew of No.2317 blows out her cylinders. These three almost timeless pictures were made by photographer Wilton Tifft in 1990. No.2317 once operated out of Winnipeg, Manitoba.*

LEFT: *More seemingly timeless pictures, these made recently on the Nevada Northern Ry. of Ely, Nevada, by Joel Jensen. The Nevada Northern was originally built in the deserts of east-central Nevada to haul copper ore and to provide general transportation for the isolated towns that supported the mines and smelters. Today, the line operates from East Ely as the Nevada Northern Railway Museum with much of the original facilities and equipment intact. No.40, a trim little engine built for passenger service, is here framed in the doorway of an abandoned desert cabin at Lane City.*

RIGHT: *Engineer T.J. Lani pauses with No.93, a freight engine, at East Ely. The front of No.40 is in the foreground. A canvas cab-awning was essential on many western locomotives, to shield against the summer sun.*

LEFT: *Engine No.93 backs slowly into the Nevada Northern's enginehouse at East Ely, with Harold Hockett guiding the move from the tender's rear stirrup.*

RIGHT: *Photographer Jensen captures No.93 firing up, just east of the enginehouse, with a loading bucket in the foreground resting in the brambles.*

BELOW: *Nevada Northern ore cars are seen from passenger car No.5. With original leaded glass and brass fittings, car No.5 is one of two vintage wooden coaches on NN.*

LEFT: *A dwindling number of the larger US rail carriers runs occasional steam excursions. In August 1991, former Norfolk & Western locomotive No.1218 heads a special excursion train past an abandoned coal tipple on the Norfolk Southern Ry. at Panther, West Virginia. No.1218 is a 6000 hp, N&W Class-A, one of the most advanced steam designs ever conceived. The front of the locomotive has a fresh coat of heat-resistant graphite. Sadly, Norfolk Southern ended its steam program in 1994.*

RIGHT: *One of the gems of historic railway preservation is the Mid-Continent Railway Museum at North Freedom, Wisconsin, with its authentically restored cars and engines. Here, MCRM's former Chicago & North Western 'Ten-Wheeler' No.1385 crosses a street in LaRue, Wis., in 1989.*

BELOW: *In summer 1988, former Reading Railroad engine No.2102, a 'Northern' type now operated by the tourist-carrying Blue Mountain & Reading, speeds an excursion train past abandoned factory buildings in Lebanon, Pa. The tracks to the right are being pulled up for salvaged rail and ties.*

LEFT: *The very picture of an immaculately restored steamer: former Great Western Ry. No.90 now owned by the Strasburg Rail Road, Strasburg, Pa., and here as overhauled in the 1970s. 'The Strasburg' is one of the pioneer steam tourist railroads.*

RIGHT: *The engineer's 'office,' in a study by John Helbok. This is former Great Western No.60, owned today by the Black River & Western Railroad of Ringoes, New Jersey. The boiler idles at 150 psi; throttle is the diagonal lever; two brake handles are at lower right; water glass and 'gauge cocks' are at upper left.*

BELOW: *On the Valley Railroad in Essex, Connecticut, something remarkable: a brand-new steamer, built in China in early 1989 and put into service by master mechanic David Conrad.*

LEFT: *Engine No.148 gets oiled on the Black River & Western, in a John Helbok photo from 1971.*

LOWER LEFT: *Engineer Seth Corwin gets engine No.2317 underway at Steamtown.*

UPPER RIGHT: *The running gear of Norfolk & Western No.1218 (p.124) in 1991, as groomed by steam crew members Doug Karhan, Bob Yuill, Bob Saxtan, Scott Lindsay and Don Pate.*

LOWER RIGHT: *Young Oren Helbok steam cleans a former Canadian Pacific locomotive on the tourist Allegheny Central Ry. in the early 1970s.*

LEFT: *After repairs to East Broad Top locomotive No.14 (see p.61) at the EBT shops in Rockhill Furnace, Pennsylvania, in 1987, mechanic Kelly Anderson drains the steam-driven air pumps for the engine's brake system, as boiler pressure is raised from a new fire.*

ABOVE: *Anderson (right) assists master mechanic Linn Moedinger in carefully placing a freshly-machined journal box and bearing onto a driving axle of EBT engine No.14 in 1987. Moedinger and Anderson are from the Strasburg Rail Road, working here for EBT.*

RIGHT: *Engineer Lloyd Arkinstall (left) and fireman Tom Davis chat on the deck of Black River & Western locomotive No.60 at the Flemington, New Jersey, station in the 1970s. The fire has been prepared, and running-gear inspection and oiling completed.*

BELOW: *Master mechanic Bob Michele (right) operates one of two big air jacks, assisted on the bar by the author, during removal of the driving wheels of former Long Island Rail Road engine No.35 in 1978 in Eisenhower Park, East Meadow, Long Island.*

LEFT: *Against a stormy sky, Canadian Pacific rails carry a special excursion with preserved CP engine Nos 136 and 1057 double-heading near Alton, Ontario, in October, 1973.*

ABOVE: *Former Grand Trunk Western locomotive No.5629, owned by Dick Jensen, is fired up in a roundhouse in Chicago, 1967. In a tragic sequence of errors, this fine engine was scrapped in 1987.*

BELOW: *On a summer evening in 1966, George Hart's former Canadian Pacific engine No.972 awaits departure at Delta, Pa, for a special run on the Maryland & Pennsylvania RR.*

LEFT: *Engine No.614, built for the Chesapeake & Ohio Railway in 1948 and today owned by entrepreneur Ross Rowland, Jr., rolls onto a turntable at Hinton, West Virginia in January, 1985, while an abandoned concrete coal tipple stands watch. No.614 is a 'Greenbrier' type, a variation on the 'Northern,' and is one of the last steam engines manufactured in the US. In 1985, No.614 ran as '614-T' in a series of road tests between Huntington, West Va, and Hinton with special instrumentation by Foster-Wheeler Corp. to study locomotive performance. The study was part of the 'ACE 3000' design project, an attempt in the 1980s to develop a new type of environmentally compatible, coal-burning locomotive which could compete in operational qualities with modern diesels. While the 'ACE 3000' project did not succeed, No.614 still operates occasionally on exhibition.*

RIGHT: *As a good example of steam locomotive preservation and operation, here is former Great Western Ry. No.60 (see p.36), now Black River & Western No.60, accelerating along the old Belvidere-Delaware Division of the Pennsylvania Railroad near Lambertville, New Jersey, with a special run in March 1977. Passengers lean out of the coach windows of the five-car train.*

LEFT: *One of the 'original' excursion engines: Southern Railway No.4501, restored by Du Pont engineer Paul Merriman and the volunteers of the Tennessee Valley Railroad Museum in 1966. The author hand-fired No.4501 with twelve coaches from Manassas up to Linden, Virginia, in 1975.*

BELOW: *Possibly the grandest steam restoration ever: former Southern Pacific No.4449, one of the Daylight engines (see p.30). Under engineer and mechanic Doyle McCormack, No.4449 was rebuilt in 1975 for the 'American Freedom Train' and has run ever since. Here she is in Oregon in 1981.*

RIGHT: *In the late 1960s and 1970s, the Southern Railway ran frequent excursions with several engines. Here are locomotive Nos 722 and 4501 with a train near Yemassee, South Carolina, running on the Seaboard Coast Line. Each engine has an extra water tender, for extended operating range.*

LEFT: *Logging locomotives have been restored as well. An outstanding example is the Cass Scenic Railroad, of Cass, West Virginia, managed as a state park. To the left is a 'Heisler' and to the right are two 'Shays,' ready to run for park visitors.*

LOWER LEFT: *Two of the oldest steamers to run actively were former Pennsylvania Railroad engine Nos 1223 and 7002, built in 1905 and 1902, respectively, and operated by the Strasburg Rail Road. Here, engineers Linn Moedinger (in No.7002) and Jim Rice (in No.1223) run together on the Conrail mainline in 1987. Retired in 1990, the engines are today exhibited at the Railroad Museum of Pennsylvania, the state museum in Strasburg.*

UPPER RIGHT: *One of the finest 'grass roots' restorations is that of St Louis Southwestern Railway No.819, rebuilt by an army of volunteers in Pine Bluff, Arkansas. 'Here she comes' in June, 1990, polished and pretty, with her beautiful train in tow.*

LOWER RIGHT: *Pennsy's K4-type is a storied part of American railroad history. K4 No.1361 was once displayed at the Horseshoe Curve near Altoona, Pennsylvania. Here, in June, 1987, after restoration by master mechanic Doyle McCormack and a crew of volunteers from the Railroaders' Memorial Museum of Altoona, No.1361 and a nine-car train arrive in Bellefonte, Pa., as North Shore Railroad president Dick Robey waves from the gangway. The first 'car' is a rail-diesel car temporarily spliced into the train; oversize flags carry Conrail and Pennsy emblems.*

LEFT: *For a time in the 1970s, Canadian National Railways ran restored locomotive No.6060 on special trips. Engines of this class were called 'Bullet-nosed Bettys' for their conical boiler fronts – and for their speed. The* author accompanied the crew at 80mph in this engine's cab, from Niagara Falls to Toronto, Ontario. Here we see the engine at Toronto on a September morning in 1973, fresh from the shop and ready to roll.

ABOVE: *Linda Simms, mainline engineer on the Southern Pacific, runs one of the two steam switching locomotives at the California State Railroad Museum, Sacramento, in 1985 in this Shirley Burman photograph.*

ABOVE: *Steam lives on, in counterpoint to our microchip age. East Broad Top Railroad's 'Fall Spectacular' in 1987 was just that, with four locomotives under steam. In this Jeff Tinsley photo,* *EBT engines 12 ('Millie'), 14 (just rebuilt), 15, and 17 run as a remarkable 'quadruple-header', bound for Orbisonia and Rockhill, Pennsylvania, from Colgate Grove, with whistles in jubilation.*

BIBLIOGRAPHY

Many handsome books have been published over the years featuring photography of the steam railroad in the twentieth century. Here are some author's recommendations:

John W. Adams, *Great Railroad Photographs: From the Collection of the Smithsonian Institution* (1994); Don Ball, Jr., *Portrait of the Rails: From Steam to Diesel* (1972), *Railroads: An American Journey* (1975), and *America's Colorful Railroads* (1978, reprinted 1987); Lucius Beebe and Charles Clegg, *The Age of Steam* (1957) and *Great Railroad Photographs, U.S.A.* (1964); Preston Cook and Jim Boyd, *The Railroad Night Scene* (1991); Donald Duke, *Night Train* (1961); James Gallagher and Jacques Kelly, *Trackside Maryland: From Railyard to Main Line* (1992); Victor Hand and Harold Edmonson, *The Love of Trains: Steam and Diesel Locomotives in Action Around the World* (1974); Frank Kyper (with William Stewart), *Philip Ross Hastings: The Boston & Maine – A Photographic Essay* (1989); O. Winston Link, *Steam, Steel and Stars* (1987); David P. Morgan, *Canadian Steam!* (1961); David P. Morgan (with Phil Hastings), *The Mohawk That Refused to Abdicate and Other Tales* (1975); David P. Morgan (with John Gruber), *Locomotive 4501* (1968, reprinted 1973); David Plowden, *A Time of Trains* (1987); Richard Steinheimer, *Backwoods Railroads of the West* (1963) and *Growing Up With Trains*, Vols. I and II (1982 and 1983); Richard Steinheimer and Don Sims, *Western Trains* (1965). A fine short history of photographers and the railroad is *Focus on Rails* by John Gruber (1989). Both historical and contemporary photography of the railroad is featured every month in the magazines *Trains, Railfan & Railroad*, and *Locomotive & Railway Preservation*. For an overview of railroad history and its social significance in the nineteenth and twentieth centuries, see Withuhn (ed.) with John Armstrong, Jim Dilts, H. Roger Grant, Walter Gray, John Hankey, and Don Hofsommer, *Rails Across America: A History of Railroads in North America* (1993).

William L. Withuhn

PICTURE CREDITS AND ACKNOWLEDGEMENTS

AAR: Association of American Railroads; **C & NW**: Chicago & North Western; **Col**: Collection; **M**: courtesy of Marian Hastings; **Md**: Maryland; **N & W**: Norfolk & Western; **Ry**: Railway.

Front endpaper: Philip Hastings, M; **1/2 title page**: Wilton Tifft; **2**: Ron Ziel; **4**: Oren Helbok; **6**: Bob Patterson; **7**: Frank Quin/Ron Ziel Col; **8**: Richard Kindig; **9**: Ron Ziel; **10**: Richard Kindig; **11**: Joel Jensen; **12-13**: Frank Quin/Ron Ziel Col; **14**: Southern Railway Historical Association Col (T); Nicholas Morant/Canadian Pacific Limited (B); **15**: Ron Ziel Col (T); Great Northern Ry (B); **16**: H.L. Broadbelt Collection; **17**: Richard Kindig (T); Frank Quin/Ron Ziel Col (B); **18-19**: Richard Kindig; **20**: Minnesota Historical Society (T); Canadian Pacific Limited (B); **21**: Southern Ry Historical Association/Women and the American Railroad Research (T); Minnesota Historical Society (B); **22-23**: AAR; **24**: AAR (T); Salamander Books (BL); **25**: Frank Quin/Ron Ziel Col (T); Ron Ziel Col (B); **26**: N & W Ry/Kenneth Miller Col (T); Jeff Winslow/Ron Ziel Col (B); **27**: Jeff Winslow/Ron Ziel Col (T); AAR (BR); **28**: AAR/Southern Pacific Company (T); **29**: Richard Kindig (T); **28-29**: Florida East Coast Railway/Seth Bramson Col; **30**: Nicholas Morant/Canadian Pacific Ltd (T); AAR/Southern Pacific Co. (B); **31**: AAR/Canadian Pacific Ltd; **32-33**: James Gallagher; **34**: Smithsonian Institution (T); FR Dirkes/Ron Ziel Col (B); **35-36**: Richard Kindig; **37**: AAR/CW Witbeck; **38**: FG Zahn (T); James Gallagher (B); **39**: AAR/Northern Pacific Railroad (T); James Gallagher (B); **40-41, 42-43**: Ron Ziel; **44-45**: AAR/Western Md Ry; **46**: Richard Kindig (T); Frank Quin/Ron Ziel Col (B); **47**: AAR/C & NW Ry (T); Richard Kindig (B); **48**: Richard Kindig (T); Frank Quin/Ron Ziel Col (B); **49**: AAR/Canadian Pacific Ltd; **50**: AAR/Canadian Pacific Ltd (T); Frank Quin/Ron Ziel Col (B); **51**: AAR/Southern Pacific Company (T); Richard Kindig (B); **52**: Norfolk Southern Corporation (T); **53**: AAR/Illinois Central Railroad (T); Ron Ziel Col (B); **54**: Richard Kindig (T); AAR/Illinois Central Railroad (B); **55**: Richard Steinheimer; **56**: Richard Kindig; **57**: AAR/Seaboard Air Line Railroad (T); John Gruber (B); **58-60**: Glen Beier; **61**: Ron Ziel (T); John Helbok (B); **62**: Richard Steinheimer (T); Smithsonian Institution (B); **63**: Joel Jensen; **64**: Richard Steinheimer; **65**: Glenn Beier (T); AAR/Farm Security Administration (B); **66**: Ron Ziel; **67**: John Gruber; **68-69**: James Gallagher; **70**: FR Dirkes/Ron Ziel Col (T); Ted Wurm/Ron Ziel Col (B); **71**: Canadian Pacific Ltd (T); Philip Hastings, M (B); **72**: Canadian Pacific Ltd (T); **72-73**: Canadian Pacific Ltd (B); **73**: AAR/Chesapeake & Ohio Ry (T); **74**: Canadian National (T); Minnesota Historical Society (B); **75**: Southern Railway Historical Association (T); Union Pacific Museum Collection (B); **76**: AAR/Pennsylvania Railroad (T); Ron Ziel Col (B); **77**: AAR/Pennsylvania Railroad; **78**: Norfolk Southern Corp/Southern Railway; **79**: Ron Ziel Col (T); AAR/Boston & Maine Railroad (B); **80-81**: N & W Ry/Kenneth L Miller Collection; **82**: Canadian Pacific Ltd; **83**: Canadian Pacific Ltd (T); AAR/Southern Pacific Co (B); **84**: Union Pacific Museum Collection (T); Minnesota Historical Society (B); **85**: Altoona Area Public Library; **86**: Railroaders' Memorial Museum, Altoona (T); Philip Hastings, M (B); **87**: John Gruber; **88**: B & O Railroad Museum/ Chesapeake & Ohio Ry; **89**: Philip Hastings, M (T); Women and the American Railroad Research (BL); Richard Steinheimer (BR); **90**: Ron Ziel (T); Canadian National (B); **91**: AAR/New York Central Railroad; **92-93**: Norfolk Southern Corp/Southern Ry; **94**: AAR/Santa Fe Ry (T); Philip Hastings, M (B); **95**: Glen Beier; **96**: Glen Beier (T); Jim Shaughnessy (B); **97**: Canadian National (T); Philip Hastings, M (B); **98-99**: Richard Steinheimer; **100**: Ron Ziel; **101**: John Krause/Ron Ziel Col (T); Ron Ziel (B); **102-103**: Richard Steinheimer; **104**: AAR/Erie Railroad; **105**: JV Osborne/Ron Ziel Col (TL); Union Pacific Museum Collection (TR); Canadian Pacific Ltd (B); **106**: Philip Hastings, M (T); Union Pacific Museum Collection (B); **107**: Smithsonian Institution (T); Richard Steinheimer (BL); Philip Hastings, M (BR); **108**: Union Pacific Museum Collection; **109**: Louisville & Nashville Railroad/Ron Ziel Col (T); Glenn Beier (B); **110**: Ron Ziel; **111**: Frank Quin/Ron Ziel Col; **112**: Ron Ziel; **113**: Jeff Tinsley/Smithsonian Institution; **114**: W Withuhn Col (T); Ron Ziel (B); **115**: Richard Steinheimer (T); C & NW Ry/Ron Ziel Col (B); **116-119**: Wilton Tifft; **120-123** Joel Jensen; **124-125**: Oren Helbok; **126**: John Helbok; **127**: John Helbok (T); Oren Helbok (B); **128**: John Helbok; **129**: Oren Helbok (T); John Helbok (B); **130**: Jeff Tinsley/Smithsonian Institution; **131**: Dane Malcolm (T); Kevin O'Connell (B); **132-134**: Ron Ziel; **135**: John Helbok; **136**: John Krause/Ron Ziel Col (T); Ron Ziel (B); **137**: Ron Ziel; **138**: Ron Ziel (T); John Helbok (B); **139-140**: Ron Ziel; **141**: Shirley Burman/Women and the American Railroad Research; **142**: Jeff Tinsley/Smithsonian Institution: **Back endpapers**: Philip Hastings, M.